HOW TO DRAW PORTRAITS, FACES AND HEADS

Charlotte

Mark Bergin

BOOK HOUSE

SALARIYA

© The Salariya Book Company Ltd MMX

Published in Great Britain in MMX by
Book House, an imprint of
The Salariya Book Company Ltd
25 Marlborough Place, Brighton BN1 1UB

1 3 5 7 9 8 6 4 2

Please visit our website at **www.book-house.co.uk**
or go to **www.salariya.com** for **free** electronic versions of:
You Wouldn't Want to be an Egyptian Mummy!
You Wouldn't Want to be a Roman Gladiator!
You Wouldn't Want to be a Polar Explorer!
**You Wouldn't Want to sail on a 19th-Century
   Whaling Ship!**

Author: Mark Bergin was born in Hastings in 1961.
He studied at Eastbourne College of Art and has
specialised in historical reconstructions as well as
aviation and maritime subjects since 1983. He lives
in Bexhill-on-Sea with his wife and three children.

Editor: Rob Walker

PB ISBN: 978-1-907184-28-4

A CIP catalogue record for this
book is available from the
British Library.

Printed and bound in China.
Printed on paper from
sustainable sources.

PAPER FROM
SUSTAINABLE
FORESTS

Contents

Making a start

Learning to draw is about looking and seeing. Keep practising and get to know your subject. Use a sketchbook to make quick drawings. Start by doodling, and experiment with shapes and patterns. There are many ways to draw; this book shows only some methods. Visit art galleries, look at artists' drawings, see how friends draw, but above all, find your own way.

When drawing from photos, use construction lines to help you to understand the form and relationships between the features of the head.

Using a squared-up grid can help you to keep the proportions of your drawing correct.

Try sketching friends and family at home.

Sketch people in everyday surroundings. This will help you to draw faster and to capture the main elements of a pose quickly.

Drawing materials

Try using different types of drawing paper and materials. Experiment with charcoal, wax crayons and pastels. All pens, from felt-tips to ballpoints, will make interesting marks — you could also try drawing with pen and ink on wet paper.

Pencil

Felt-tip

Hard **pencils** are greyer and soft pencils are blacker. Hard pencils are graded from 6H (the hardest) through 5H, 4H, 3H and 2H to H. Soft pencils are graded from B, 2B, 3B, 4B and 5B up to 6B (the softest).

Silhouette is a style of drawing that mainly uses only solid black shapes.

Lines drawn in **ink** cannot be erased, so keep your ink drawings sketchy and less rigid. Don't worry about mistakes as these lines can be lost in the drawing as it develops.

Ink

Charcoal is very soft and can be used for big, bold drawings. Ask an adult to spray your charcoal drawing with fixative to prevent it smudging.

You can create special effects by scraping away parts of a drawing done with **wax crayons**.

Pastels are even softer than charcoal, and come in a wide range of colours. Ask an adult to spray your pastel drawing with fixative to prevent it smudging.

7

Bones and muscles

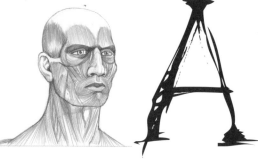

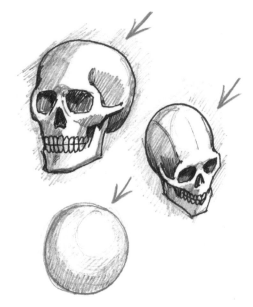

A little understanding of the shape of the skull and the muscle structure that lies under the skin can really help when drawing the human head. The outward apperance of a human head is based entirely on the underlying shape of the hard bone and muscle contours.

Here we can see the effect of a light source on the skull. Note which areas become darker as the skull changes position.

These two drawings are of the skull from a side view and a frontal view.

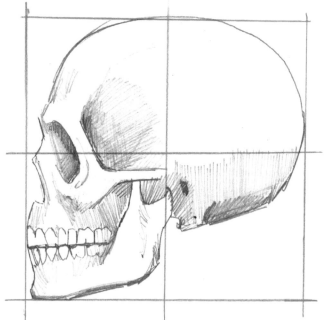

Using a grid helps you to keep the skull in proportion.

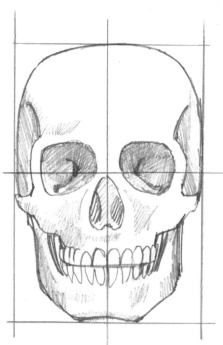

Dividing your drawing into four sections for a frontal view can help you maintain the symmetry of the skull.

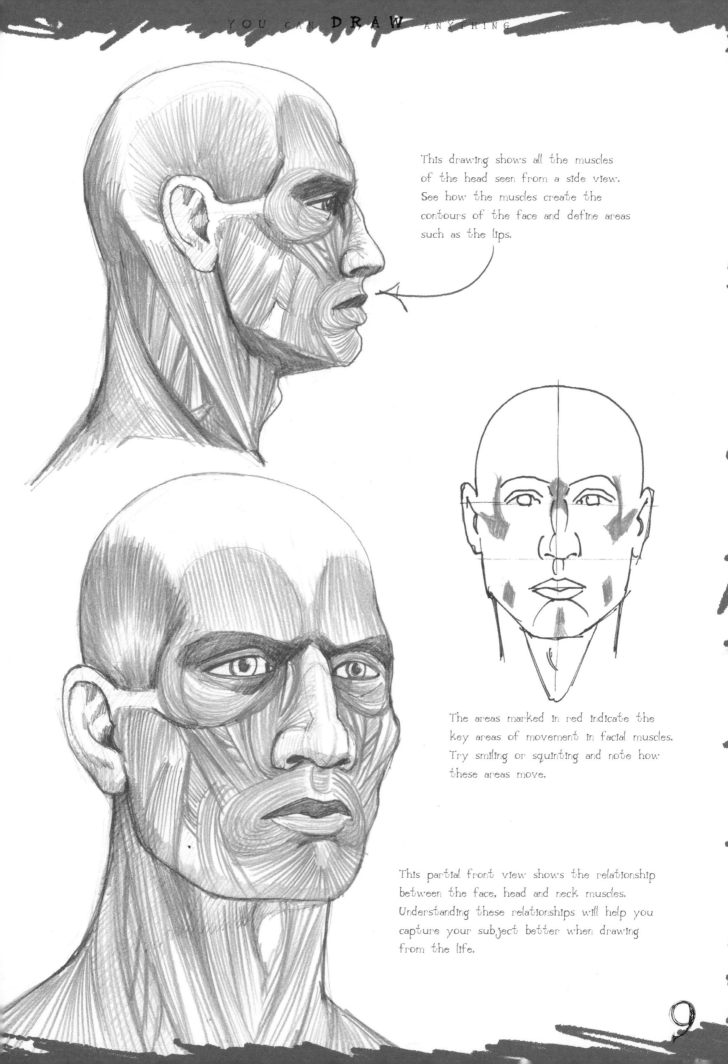

This drawing shows all the muscles
of the head seen from a side view.
See how the muscles create the
contours of the face and define areas
such as the lips.

The areas marked in red indicate the
key areas of movement in facial muscles.
Try smiling or squinting and note how
these areas move.

This partial front view shows the relationship
between the face, head and neck muscles.
Understanding these relationships will help you
capture your subject better when drawing
from the life.

9

The head

Heads are difficult shapes to draw. The face includes some of the most expressive features of the body. Using construction lines helps to place the eyes, nose, ears and mouth accurately on the head.

Frontal view

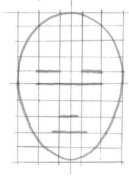

Squaring up the paper can help you with the positioning of the facial features.

Establish the main shape of the head by overlapping two ovals.

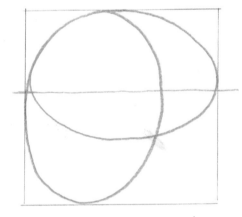

Construction lines help you to keep the features in the correct positions when drawing the head from different angles.

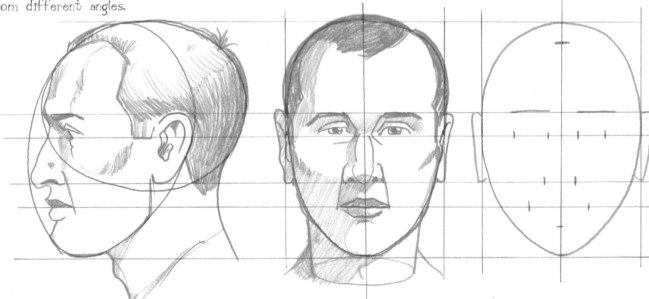

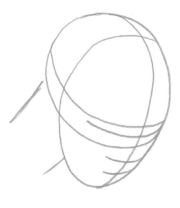

Draw construction lines to indicate the position of each facial feature.

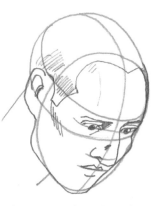

These construction lines have been used to draw a male head.

These construction lines have been used to draw a female head.

Use downward curving construction lines to show the head looking downwards.

Accurate construction lines make it much easier to draw in the facial features and details.

Use upward curving to construction lines to show the head looking up.

Draw in the features. Do not forget the underside of the chin.

Complete any details and remove unwanted construction lines.

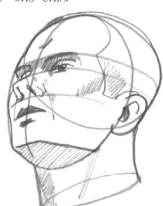

The eyes

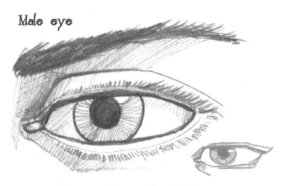

Each eyeball sits in its own socket and is protected by the eyelids. The eyes and eyebrows are very expressive.

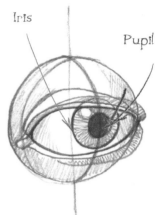

An eyeball is spherical in shape. Its most visible features are the iris and pupil. Start by drawing a spherical eyeball. Add the shape of the eyelids.

Male eye

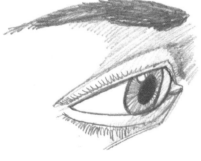

Once the visible part of the eye is drawn add detail to the iris. Always leave an area of white as a highlight.

Female eye

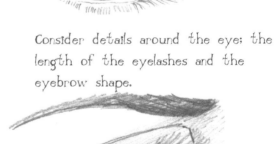

Consider details around the eye; the length of the eyelashes and the eyebrow shape.

When drawing the eye from the side it is important to use perspective.

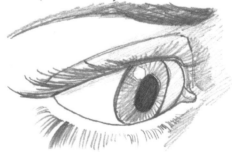

Check your light source before adding tone to the drawing. The area where the nose projects out from the eyes tends to be darker.

Eyes from below

Eyes from above

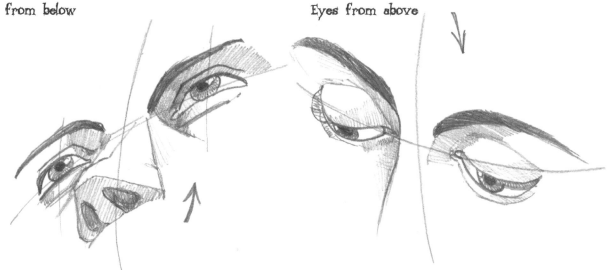

When drawing the eyes from this angle, use a downward—curving construction line to place them accurately.

Drawing the eyes from above means you see less of the eyeball.

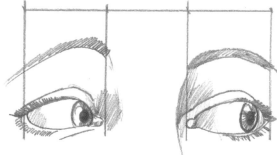

When drawing both eyes it is very important that they are both the same scale. It helps to start your drawing using carefully worked out construction lines.

It is important to consider the light source with this kind of view.

Partially shut eyelids show less of the eyeball. Add more shaded areas.

The positioning of the pupil and iris is important as it shows where the eyes are looking. Keep their direction similar.

13

The mouth

The mouth is very expressive and can give an insight into a person's mood or their emotions.

These are the basic construction lines for drawing lips from the side.

Once the construction lines are in place use them as a guide to create the tone of the lips.

Upward curving construction lines are used to draw the mouth from below.

Construction lines for a front view.

When adding tone to the lips always use lines curving into the mouth to create shape. Add more lines where more shade is needed.

Mouths can be very expressive. Practise drawing your own mouth from a variety of different angles.

Here the mouth is seen slightly open.

Add more detail to the upper teeth than the lower teeth. This looks more natural and creates more of a focal point when drawing a mouth.

Side view of mouth, biting the bottom lip.

This smile is slightly askew, showing more teeth on one side.

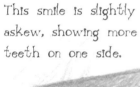

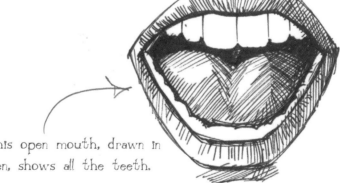

This open mouth, drawn in pen, shows all the teeth.

This mouth is open but the lips hide the teeth.

This looks like a happy expressive smile.

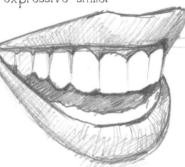

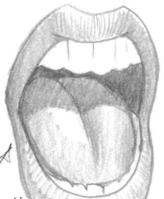

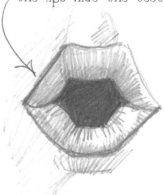

This wide open mouth is probably shouting.

Noses

Noses come in a vast variety of shapes and sizes. Drawing a nose from different angles is a key skill to learn when drawing the head.

This shows the basic areas of shading needed to give a nose its shape.

The darkest area of the nose is inside the nostril.

These construction lines help you to draw the nose from below.

These three sets of construction lines show the shape of the nose from different angles. Use this basic shape to create the nose in all shapes and sizes.

Adding tone to the nose is very important because it creates and emphasises its shape. Study the nose to see how the light hits it and add tone to clarify its shape and angle.

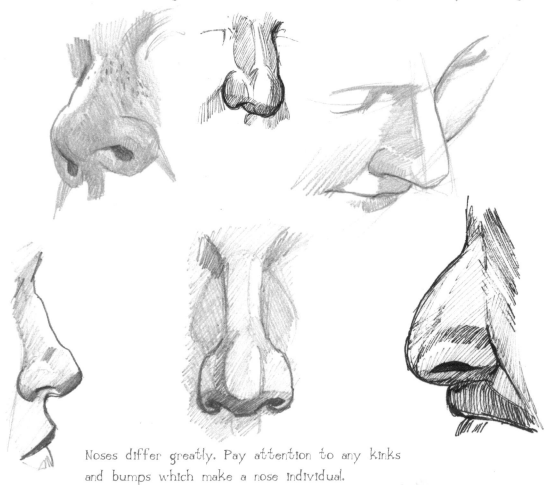

Noses differ greatly. Pay attention to any kinks and bumps which make a nose individual.

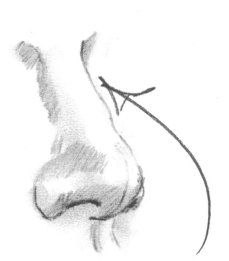

Use highlights where appropriate.

Always relate the nose to the other facial features to get the proportions right.

17

Ears

T he variation in people's ears is endless, as no two ears are the same, even on the same head. An ear is quite a complicated form and is drawn almost entirely using curved lines.

Draw the basic shape of the ear with one curved line.

Draw curved lines to create the structure.

Add tone to create a three-dimensional feel to the ear structure.

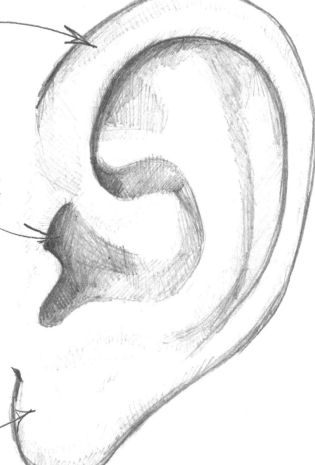

Add shading to the ear hole and its complicated folds where less light reaches.

The earlobe usually catches most of the light.

The ear comes in so many shapes and sizes. Look carefully at them when drawing a subject as the shape may be quite distinctive.

This ear has quite a rounded shape.

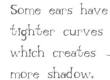

Earlobes come in many shapes and sizes. Some extend below the ear while others attach directly to the head.

Some ears have tighter curves which creates more shadow.

Ears can look very different depending on what media you draw them in.

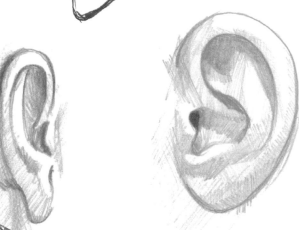

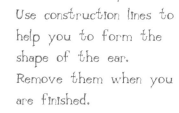

Use construction lines to help you to form the shape of the ear. Remove them when you are finished.

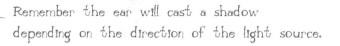

Remember the ear will cast a shadow depending on the direction of the light source.

19

Light sources

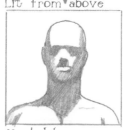

Lit from above

From the side

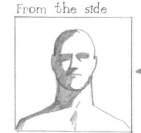

No lighting

From below

The effect of different light sources.

The light source for a drawing can have a huge effect on the finished picture. Placing your model beside a well-lit window or another strong light source will give you stark contrasts to create a dynamic image.

The face is drawn with its light source from the right, casting the left side of the face into shadow.

← Light source.

This drawing is done in white chalk on black paper. Use highlights instead of shading to create the shape of the face. Note exactly how the light source hits the subject.

Light source

Use the negative effect of drawing with a light material on dark paper to give your drawing added drama.

Light source

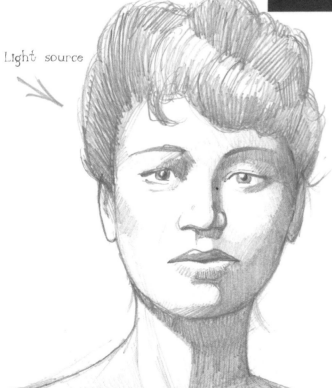

Light source

Light source

Light source

When light hits a domed surface, shading must be applied gradually from light to dark.

21

Young people

Drawing a child's head is very different from drawing an adult head. The proportions of the face and head change quite considerably.

Draw two overlapping ovals for the shape of the head.

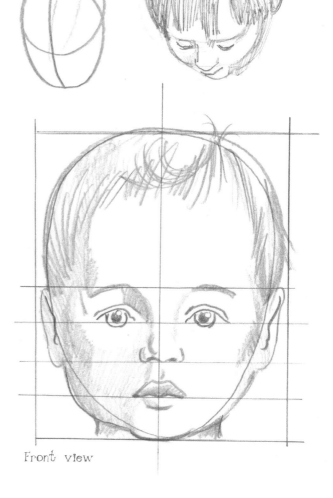

Construction lines help you to measure the head's features and proportions.

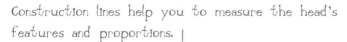

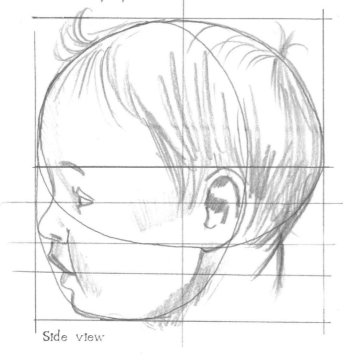

Side view

Front view

Practise drawing children's heads in many different positions.

Use construction lines to help proportion and position features.

Draw in the hair shape using simple, flowing lines.

Sketch in the facial features and other details.

Ink line drawings can be very effective. Keep the lines simple — do not overwork or you will age the features.

A sleeping child is a great subject to draw.

23

The elderly

As people age their facial features become more exaggerated and distinct. The face gradually acquires folds, wrinkles and lines. This can make a person fascinating to draw.

This brow shows many wrinkles and lines; details which define an elderly person's portrait.

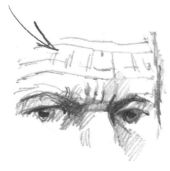

Note the detail around the eye. 'Crows' feet' spread from the outer corners of each eye.

Add more lines around the mouth to suggest wrinkles.

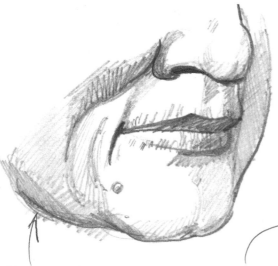

Add curved lines under the chin and around the throat to show the effect of aging skin

Lines around the nose are more pronounced than on a younger person.

This simple ink line drawing uses no tone but still suggests age through its careful use of curved lines.

When drawing someone who is balding, study the shape of the hairline carefully.

In old age the structure of the face becomes more delineated but colour fades. Eyebrows, hair and lips become less defined.

This portrait relies on heavy patched tone to convey the age of the subject.

25

Expressions

OF acial expressions can convey an enormous insight into a person's emotions or reactions.

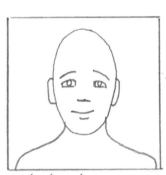

Using a mirror
Try looking at your drawing in a mirror. Seeing it in reverse can help you spot mistakes.

These small thumbnail sketches show a simple guide to everyday facial expressions.

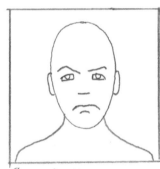
Laughter

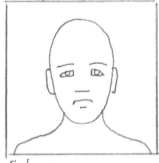
Grumpiness

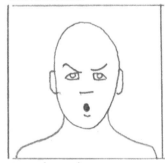
Contentment

Anger

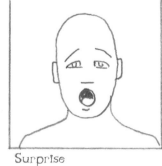
Sadness

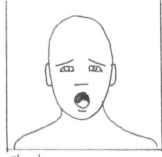
Puzzlement

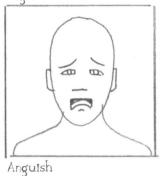
Anguish

Surprise

Shock

26

Always start your drawing of a head with two overlapping ovals to get the shape right.

Refer to the simple guides to help you create the expression you want. Then build up the features and add details.

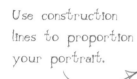

Use construction lines to proportion your portrait.

Note that certain expressions can wrinkle the skin, causing temporary lines.

27

Self-portraits

Self-portraits have been done throughout the history of art. Great artists such as Da Vinci, Rembrandt, Picasso and Van Gogh have all left impressions of themselves in drawings and paintings.

Da Vinci

Rembrandt

Picasso

Van Gogh

Light source

Draw yourself in a mirror to practise drawing portraits. Use a good light source such as a window and remember that your drawing will be in reverse.

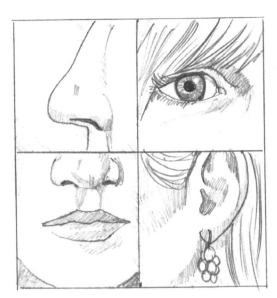

Try concentrating on particular details of your face, like the eye or nose for example. These could the be arranged together to form an interesting composition.

Create an interesting line drawing. Study a photograph of yourself and try to recognise your most defining features. Now trace the photograph and try to capture your likeness with as few lines as possible.

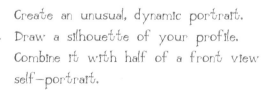

Create an unusual, dynamic portrait. Draw a silhouette of your profile. Combine it with half of a front view self-portrait.

Accessories

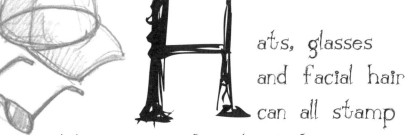ats, glasses and facial hair can all stamp personality on a subject. Each can give a valuable insight into what defines a person's identity.

Always use construction lines when adding accessories to check the proportions.

When adding glasses, take care to position them correctly on the nose and ears.

Take care to get the overall shape of the beard correct. Draw in lots of short lines to show the direction of the hairs.

Negative Space

Always check the negative space — the area around your drawing. This can help you spot mistakes.

Beards can cover large areas of the chin. Start by drawing in the chin line before adding a beard.

Hats come in many shapes and sizes, and sit on the head in different ways.

Draw circular construction lines to position the hat correctly on the head.

Consider the width and height of the hat and make sure it fits around the head.

Remember that a hat brim will cast a shadow over the face.

Hats can be worn at all angles, which can help you to capture a person's character.

Caps sit very tight on the head and only cast a shadow on the front of the face.

31

Glossary

Composition The arrangement of the parts of a picture on the drawing paper.

Construction lines Guidelines used in the early stages of a drawing, and usually erased later.

Fixative A type of resin used to spray over a finished drawing to prevent smudging. **It should only be used by an adult.**

Light source The direction from which the light seems to come in a drawing.

Perspective A method of drawing in which near objects are shown larger than faraway objects to give an impression of depth.

Pose The position assumed by a figure.

Proportion The correct relationship of scale between each part of the drawing.

Silhouette A drawing that shows only a flat dark shape, like a shadow.

Vanishing point The place in a perspective drawing where parallel lines appear to meet.

Index